THE
FOLK

STENCIL BOOK

A UNIQUE COLLECTION OF READY-TO-USE STENCILS
IN CLASSIC DESIGNS BY

LOUISE DRAYTON
JANE THOMSON

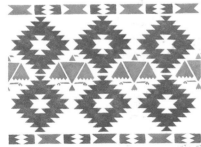

HOW TO BEGIN PP. 2–7

TROPICAL AFRICAN PP. 8–11

DESERT AFRICAN PP. 12–15

MOORISH PP. 16–19

NATIVE AMERICAN PP. 20–23

MAYAN & AZTEC PP. 24–27

MIX & MATCH PP. 28–31

DK

DK PUBLISHING, INC.

D1361170

How to Begin

STENCILING IS AN ANCIENT DECORATIVE technique and is easy to master. Once you understand how to do it, you will find that stenciling a pattern takes very little time. First, choose your design. Then measure the surface you want to stencil and decide how and where to use the pattern. Experiment with different colors and backgrounds to give your design another look, and try masking and combining other motifs with your stencil to build a unique design. You can use your stencils just about anywhere, and – with a little imagination – create hundreds of designs.

STARTING TO STENCIL

BEFORE YOU BEGIN any project, start with a simple design and practice on shelf paper. Begin with the dry stages: gather the equipment you will need, and then cut your sponges and stencils. Mask the edges of the stencil. Next, the wet stages: experiment with paint consistency and sponging, then practice dabbing on scrap paper.

SHELF PAPER

PLUMB LINE

HOME-MADE PLUMB LINE

LARGE RULER

TRY SQUARE

Make your own plumb line with a small weight and string

EMULSION

METALLIC PAINT

SOLVENT

TUBE ACRYLIC

FABRIC MEDIUM

STUCCO PAINT AND SPATULA

ACRYLICS

CERAMIC PAINTS

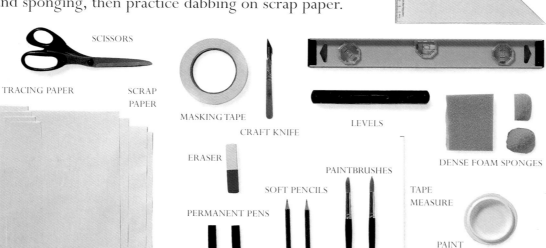

SCISSORS

TRACING PAPER

SCRAP PAPER

MASKING TAPE

CRAFT KNIFE

LEVELS

DENSE FOAM SPONGES

ERASER

PAINTBRUSHES

SOFT PENCILS

TAPE MEASURE

PERMANENT PENS

PAINT DISHES

STENCILING EQUIPMENT
Stenciling tools include a pair of scissors, sponge, tape, ruler, pen, soft pencils, paper, paint and dish, and paintbrush. More complex projects need additional materials.

1 Cut the sponge into 1½-in and 2½-in (35-mm and 65-mm) squares; trim off the tops to create a smooth dome shape. Make a few smaller domes for fine detail.

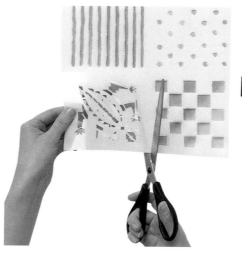

2 Working on a flat surface, trace the guidelines from the page behind each plastic stencil sheet with indelible ink; cut out and number each stencil.

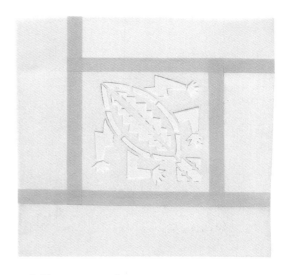

3 Tape strips of tracing paper 2 in (5 cm) wide to each side to prevent paint from smudging over your surface. Cover parts of the stencil you will not need (see p.6).

Watery paint will drip off your sponge and can ruin your stencil design

The paint should be the consistency of cream

Too much thick paint makes a dense, heavy color with no pattern marks from the sponge

Watery paint creates a washed-out color with small bubbles

This paint is at the right consistency to produce a textured pattern

4 *It is very important that your paint is mixed to a creamy consistency. Bottled acrylics should be about right, but you may have to thin other types of paint.*

5 *Test the consistency of your paints by dabbing the sponge lightly onto scrap paper. Paint of the right consistency will produce an evenly stippled texture.*

WATERY PAINT

The paint shown here is too watery and, because it has seeped under the stencil, all the details are lost — a disastrous result.

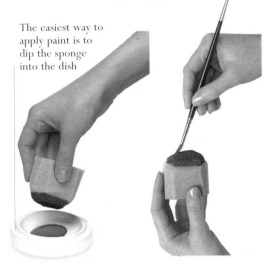

The easiest way to apply paint is to dip the sponge into the dish

This paint has not been worked evenly into the sponge, producing a blotchy texture

Coverage is better, but dabbing on the same spot would work the paint in

This paint has been applied well and the texture is uniform

6 *Apply a little paint to the rounded dome of a dry sponge. There are two ways to do this. You can dab the sponge lightly into a dish of paint, or use a brush to coat the sponge.*

7 *Before doing your stencil, dab the sponge onto scrap paper to work in all the excess paint. Dab gently in one area, and then below to test.*

8 *The sponge dome must be smooth and evenly coated with paint to produce an even texture with no blotches.*

Each time you add more paint to the sponge, re-test the distribution of paint

Make sure the paint is dry before repositioning the stencil

9 *Tape down the stencil on shelf or scrap paper to practice. Dab a sponge over the whole pattern with the first color; use a clean, dry sponge for the second color to add depth or to pick out areas of detail.*

10 *When you have applied all your chosen colors, slowly peel back the stencil to check paint texture and distribution.*

USING YOUR STENCILS

Choosing a pattern is the first step in using your stencils. Decide where you want to use your design and select your color scheme. Do you want a bold all-over pattern, a bright picture rail, or a striking motif to act as a focal point in a room? Depending on your choices, you may need to master a variety of techniques, such as measuring, repeating, and mitering. After you have completed a project, clean your stencils, repair any damage, and store the stencils flat for the next use. With care, your stencils will last a long time, and can be used again and again.

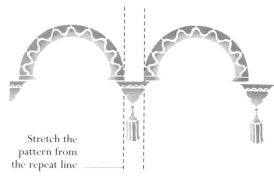

MEASURING THE PATTERN

Before you apply a pattern to any surface, stencil a sample on shelf paper as a guide. Mark the center line and the base-line of the main part of the design on the shelf paper, then mark and measure the distance to the pattern's repeat.

Mark the horizontal baseline of the main part of the design – use a level to help you keep the pattern even

This distance is the pattern repeat length

Use a plumb line to keep the stencil true

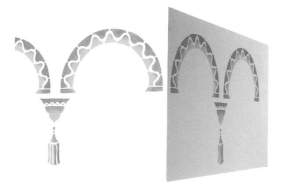

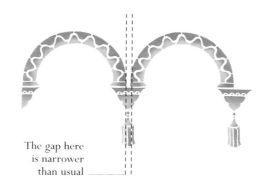

The gap here is narrower than usual

Stretch the pattern from the repeat line

SPACING THE PATTERN

Measure your surface and work out the number of repeats. Avoid stenciling on a corner by adding space between the repeats.

CLOSING UP THE PATTERN

You may need to alter the pattern to make it fit your surface; to include more repeats, close up the space between them.

STRETCHING THE PATTERN

Leave wider gaps between parts of the stencil or between repeats to stretch it; these gaps should be the same throughout the design.

Stencil a continuous border just below the ceiling if you want to make it seem lower

A boxlike motif is particularly easy to miter around a door or window

A large design flanked by another pattern repeated on each side creates a dramatic, harmonious look

Use an existing picture rail as a guide for positioning your design – or stencil a picture rail

Create a dado and enliven a room with a stencil placed about 3 ft (90 cm) above the floorboards

Repeat a bold design around a door or in a hallway; vary the height to suit the space

Make the most of baseboards by stenciling a bright pattern just above them

STENCILING A ROOM

Planning ahead is essential if you are considering an overall stenciling plan. Sketch your room, draw in your ideas, and hang practice stencils to judge their effect and color. If you intend to stencil for several hours, add a slow-dry medium to your paints to keep them usable for longer .

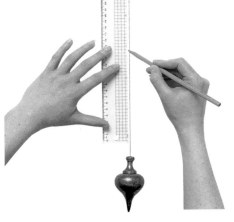

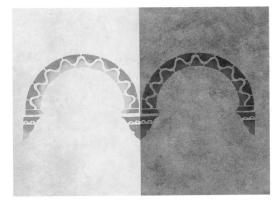

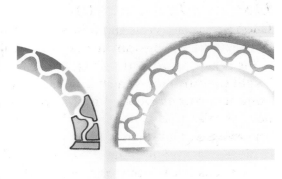

ALIGNING PATTERNS

If you need a vertical rule to align a stencil, hang a plumb line above the stencil area, place a ruler against the string, and draw a line with pencil or chalk; erase the line later.

TESTING DIFFERENT COLORS

Check that you like the colors for your design by stenciling onto a sample of your wall color or wallpaper. Depending on the background, colors can appear different.

EQUAL SPACING

Position a second stencil so that the tracing-paper mask around the stencil overlaps the first. Trace a few lines. Stencil, place the third stencil, and match tracings with the second.

MITERING

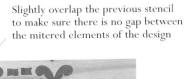
Place the set square at the point where horizontal and vertical baselines intersect

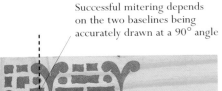
Slightly overlap the previous stencil to make sure there is no gap between the mitered elements of the design

Successful mitering depends on the two baselines being accurately drawn at a 90° angle

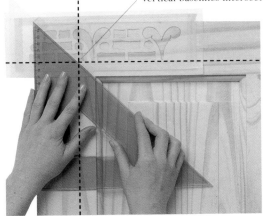

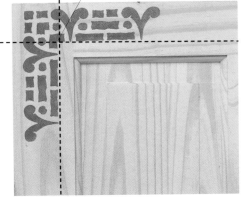

1 Working from penciled baselines, use a try square to position a tracing-paper mask at 45° across the end of the stencil. Tape it to the stencil, and dab in paint.

2 Finish the horizontal pattern, then blot the stencil, keeping the mask in place. Flip the stencil, position it on the vertical baseline, and dab in paint.

3 Carefully peel back the stencil when the paint is dry. After you remove the stencil, rub out the horizontal and vertical baselines with a very soft eraser.

CARING FOR YOUR STENCILS

Stencils are delicate and need to be handled with care. Remove tape and masks gently, and clean the stencils after each use. The inked numbers may rub off, so renew them as needed. Store each stencil flat between sheets of paper.

1 Clean off dried acrylic paints with a special acrylic solvent. Use a paintbrush to ease off the paint.

2 Soak the stencils in warm soapy water, and rinse in clean water. Dry them flat between light cotton towels.

REPAIRING DAMAGED STENCILS

Some of the stencil designs are very intricate, and they may develop small rips or tears if the stencils are not handled properly. This type of damage is easy to repair.

1 Start by covering the tear on both sides of the stencil with masking tape. Be sure the stencil is perfectly flat.

2 Using a craft knife, carefully cut along the edge of the design. Peel away any excess tape.

PAINT EFFECTS

How you use your paints will completely transform the look of your stencils. Mixing colors is fun and easy – use a brush to blend them, and keep a record of the quantities you use. Try blending, highlighting, and shading, and experiment to achieve the style that suits you best.

BLENDING COLORS

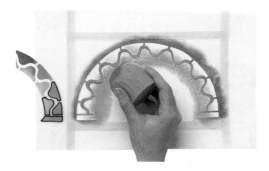

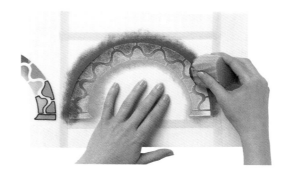

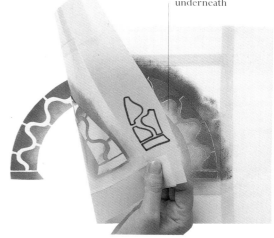

This design has been stenciled as though the light source is from underneath

1 Start by sponging the base color, which should be the lightest shade, over your first stencil. Apply the paint evenly, then add extra color to areas of fine detail.

2 Use a clean, dry sponge for your next color to avoid muddying the paints. Stipple the second deeper color lightly over the first coat; blend toward the edges.

3 When the paint is dry, remove the first stencil. If you use additional stencils, repeat Steps 1 and 2; try to match the color density and tone of the first stencil.

MASKING A STENCIL

The simplest way to create a mask is to tape a piece of tracing paper over the part of the design you will not be using. Masking allows you to isolate part of a design or color areas that need to be distinct, to simplify a complicated pattern, or to substitute one part of a stencil for another.

SIMPLE MASKING

A sheet of straight-edged paper makes an effective mask – here, a row of diamonds has been covered to create triangles

1 Start by covering the part of the design you want to mask with tracing paper. Secure the paper with tape.

2 Place the stencil in position and dab in paints. When the paint is dry, gently remove the stencil.

ADDING TEXTURE

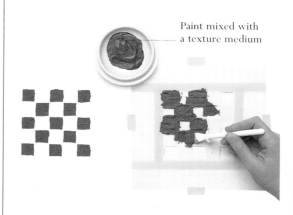

Paint mixed with a texture medium

A special medium, usually available as a gel, can be mixed in with your paint to create textured effects. Because the paint is now thicker, it is easier to apply with a small spatula instead of a brush.

THREE-IN-ONE MASKING

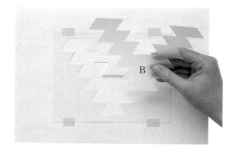

1 Some stencils in this book have three parts – two inner elements and an outer frame. Label the inner parts; use a craft knife to cut the bridges away from the outer frame.

2 Remove one of the inner elements (here, part B) to expose the area that will be filled with color. Secure part A to the outer stencil frame with tape, position, and stencil.

3 Peel back the stencil. There will now be an empty space where part A was. To fill it with color, remove A from the outer frame, attach B, reposition the frame, and stencil.

STENCILING ON OTHER MATERIALS

Almost any surface can be stenciled – from bare plaster walls to fabric, wood, ceramics, and glass. All of these can be sponged with acrylic or special paints (follow the manufacturer's instructions carefully; some ceramic paints may need to be baked). Areas that need to be protected can be varnished.

FABRICS

Stencil onto fabrics such as silk, muslin, or cotton

PAINT CONSISTENCY
Do not thin the paint you use on fabrics, as it is easier to use when thick. To prevent bleeding, add a commercial fabric medium.

USING BLOTTERS
When stenciling lightweight or sheer fabrics, such as muslin or silk, use a blotter of absorbent paper or remnants beneath the fabric in case the paint soaks through.

WOODS

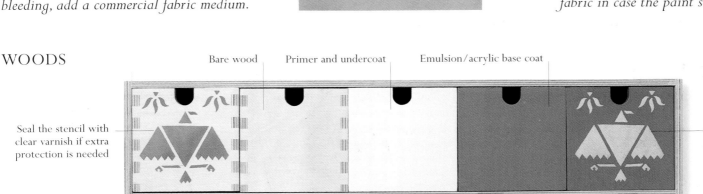

Bare wood   Primer and undercoat   Emulsion/acrylic base coat

Seal the stencil with clear varnish if extra protection is needed

Seal the board with wood primer and an undercoat, then stencil with acrylic or emulsion paints

BARE WOOD
Prepare the wood surface with sandpaper or steel wool, and wipe clean. Stencil the design. If you want a richly colored, polished effect, treat the wood with beeswax after stenciling.

PAINTED WOOD
Sand the wood before you begin. Prime it, sand the surface, paint an undercoat, then sand again. Brush after each sanding. Paint the background color; when dry, stencil your design.

CERAMICS, METAL, AND GLASS

GLASS
Stencil directly onto clean glass with ceramic paints. Fingerprints or any tape residues will prevent the paint from adhering properly.

GLAZED CERAMICS
Stencil directly onto glazed surfaces with ceramic paints (follow the manufacturer's instructions). Ceramic tiles can be stenciled either in place or when "loose" (before they have been fitted). If loose, line the tiles up, number them, and tape closely together; this will make positioning the painted tiles much easier.

UNGLAZED CERAMICS
Unglazed ceramics, such as terra-cotta pots or tiles, can be stenciled with acrylic paints.

METAL
Metallic surfaces – tin buckets, for example – can be painted with ceramic paints. With care, the design will last.

TROPICAL AFRICAN

Some of the oldest designs of this region — highly stylized, geometrical shapes, and depictions of animal bodies, markings, or tracks — are found on rock paintings, and are still used. Grids and squares were common and found on goatskin or leather cushions as well as other household items, such as brass dishes, gourds, and baskets. Sometimes even stones and large seeds were decorated. Certain designs had special meanings and were painted on the body and on houses to signify a person's identity or status, or for protection. In this environment, the calabash tree played a singular role: its large fruit was hollowed out, decorated, and used to store liquids, while the wood was cut and carved into stamping blocks for decorating fabric.

Make sure that the first stencil of any pattern sits in position — use a level to draw the horizontal line

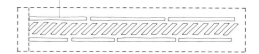

1 *Mask off the left end of Stencil 6 (see "Masking a Stencil," p.6). Use a pencil or soft chalk to mark a horizontal line and vertical line in the area to be painted, and begin to stencil at the top left-hand corner.*

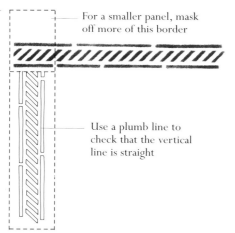

For a smaller panel, mask off more of this border

Use a plumb line to check that the vertical line is straight

2 *Turn the stencil, and place the masked end at a right angle to the top stencil. Place a try square over the stencil to check the angle, and reposition if necessary.*

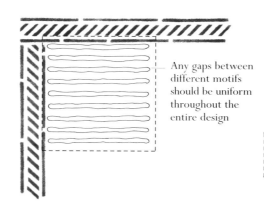

Any gaps between different motifs should be uniform throughout the entire design

3 *Position the zebra stripes (Stencil 4) in the left-hand corner. You can enlarge the design by widening the gap between the stripes and the border.*

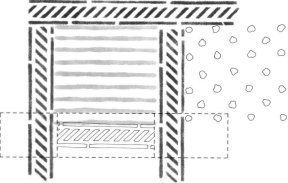

4 *After completing the stripes, stencil the border pattern to the right. Mask each end of the border pattern, place to fit between the two vertical borders, and stencil.*

The checkered square should be placed to the right and then below the leopard spots

5 *Dab in the leopard spots (Stencil 3) to the right of the border. Let the stencil dry, then dab more spots below the stripes. Stencil another vertical border.*

You can combine stencils, and use them on odd shapes, such as a lampbase. The stencils are flexible and can bend around curves.

Finish the panel with Stencil 6 along the baseline

1

2

Trace the guidelines from this page onto the plastic stencil sheet with indelible ink. Cut along the vertical line of perforations that attaches the sheet to the book. Cut out and number each stencil. Place each one on cardboard before removing any remaining infills with a craft knife.

3

4

5

6

TROPICAL AFRICAN VARIATIONS

BORDER (YORUBA TRIBE): STENCILS 4, 5

Begin with Stencil 5, then cut a mask to cover part of Stencil 4 and dab in paint

LEAF FRIEZE (KUBA TRIBE): STENCILS 2, 4

Cut an oval mask to cover the turtle's body (Stencil 2), place on stripes (Stencil 4), and stencil; mask off turtle legs and head, and stencil in empty oval

SQUARE PANEL: STENCILS 1, 3, 4, 6

Stencil this panel on a cushion cover, or enlarge it for a bedspread

BEADED BORDER: STENCILS 1, 3

TURTLE TRACKS: STENCIL 6

MOTIF BORDER: STENCILS 3, 5

CHECKERED BORDER: STENCIL 1

TURTLE FRIEZE: STENCILS 1, 2, 5

Pencil a horizontal line, and place the stripe of the turtle's back on this line

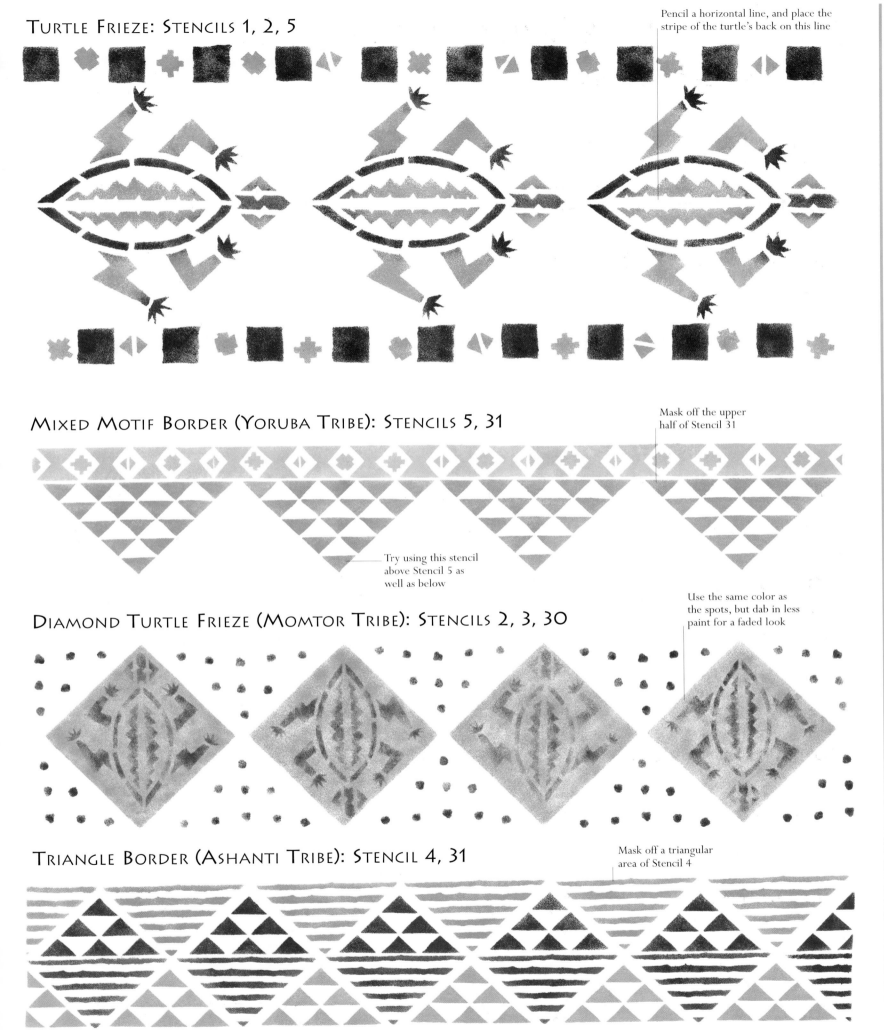

MIXED MOTIF BORDER (YORUBA TRIBE): STENCILS 5, 31

Mask off the upper half of Stencil 31

Try using this stencil above Stencil 5 as well as below

DIAMOND TURTLE FRIEZE (MOMTOR TRIBE): STENCILS 2, 3, 30

Use the same color as the spots, but dab in less paint for a faded look

TRIANGLE BORDER (ASHANTI TRIBE): STENCIL 4, 31

Mask off a triangular area of Stencil 4

DESERT AFRICAN

THE HARSH CONDITIONS OF THE DESERT have made life difficult for people living there, and many have been nomads for centuries. Traders from the Arabian peninsula established caravan routes across the Sahara through an area that now covers Algeria, Tunisia, and Morocco, bringing artifacts and design motifs with them. Outside a few larger settlements, people lived in tents, which protected them from the sun, the wind, and the cold nights. Textiles woven on hand-looms were made into woolen tent cloths, rugs, wall hangings, and blankets; these were often decorated with diamond shapes, triangles, and chevrons in broad horizontal bands. Some textiles incorporated gold and silver threads, and such valuable cloths would often form part of a bride's dowry.

Run the length of your border space with this stencil first

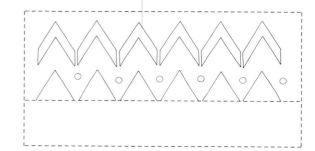

1 *Mark a horizontal line (if working on a wall, use a level). Mask off half the diamonds on Stencil 10. Place the stencil on the line, and dab with paint.*

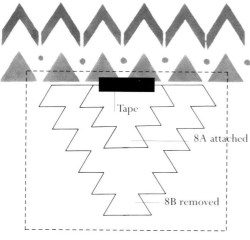

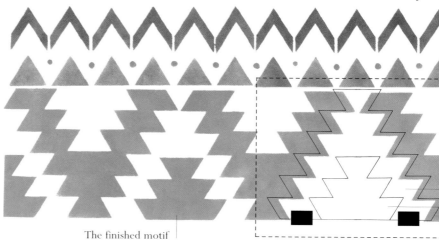

The finished motif

2 *Remove 8B (the large stepped chevron) from Stencil 8; retain 8A with tape. Place under the border.*

3 *Stencil the large stepped chevron below the entire length of the border. When paint is dry, remove 8A from the stencil.*

4 *Reattach 8B with tape, and turn the entire stencil upside down. Stencil the small stepped chevron inside the larger one.*

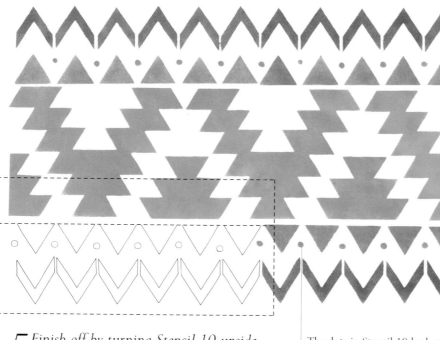

5 *Finish off by turning Stencil 10 upside down, with the mask still in place, and stencil along the length of the border.*

The dots in Stencil 10 look strong when highlighted in a color that contrasts with the border

You can create translucent colors, such as those on the back wall, by adding an extender medium to the paint; this makes it thinner and clearer without becoming watery.

7

8

A

B

Trace the guidelines from this page onto the plastic stencil sheet. Cut along the vertical line of perforations that attaches the sheet to the book. Cut out and number each stencil. Place each one on cardboard before removing any remaining infills with a craft knife.

Cut the holding bridges of Stencil 8 to create three separate parts: A, B, and the outer frame. Use tape to position A or B as needed.

9

10

Desert African Variations

Fishes: Stencil 7

Chevron Frieze: Stencils 8, 10

Position the outer frame of Stencil 8, then place 8B less than an inch away; dab in paint to create the outline shape, then stencil in the mirror image

Stepped Chevrons & Triangles: Stencils 8, 10

Choose a strong color for the dots

Diamond Zigzags: Stencil 10

This design would create a striking border for a floor rug

Four-Fishes Square: Stencils 7, 10

Mask off all but the points of the diamonds on Stencil 10 to create the frame

Dots & Diamonds: Stencil 10

Braided Band: Stencil 9

Double Zigzags: Stencil 10

Dots & Triangles: Stencil 10

Diamonds & Crosses: Stencil 9

Linked Fishes: Stencil 7

Diamonds & Fishes: Stencils 7, 10

Crosses & Chevrons: Stencils 7, 8, 9

This frieze can be used upside down or right side up, or doubled for a very wide design

MOORISH

IN THE SEVENTH CENTURY, nomadic northern African tribes were conquered by an Islamic army from the Arab world. Their descendants, the Moors, invaded Spain in 711 and created a distinctive, sophisticated culture. Moorish art, governed by Islamic principles, generally prohibited the representation of divine or saintly personages, and focused instead on highly stylized and decorative elements. Intricate designs, many derived from Arabic calligraphy, were adapted for tiles, jewelry, and clothing. Architecture was and is a vital part of Islamic culture, and Moorish arches – a key structural feature – were often decorated with embroidered textiles. Tassels, a popular decorative element, were made from the loose ends of a woven cloth tied into a knot. They were often embellished with beads and are found everywhere: on hangings, cushions, bags, clothing – even on the reins of horses and camels.

This design is extremely versatile and looks especially striking in rich colors. Try a gold or metallic paint to enrich the base color.

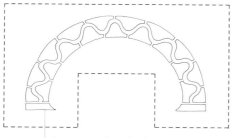

Be sure to align the bases of the stencil on an even horizontal line

1 *Using a level, mark out a horizontal line on the wall with either pencil or chalk. Place both bases of Stencil 11 on this line, and dab in paint.*

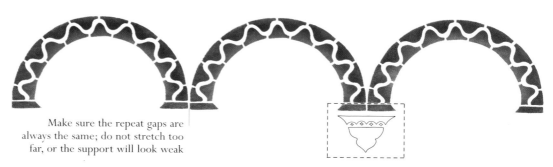

Make sure the repeat gaps are always the same; do not stretch too far, or the support will look weak

2 *Continue to stencil the arches along the horizontal line, leaving a small gap between them. This gap can be increased if you want to stretch the design slightly.*

3 *Once you have completely finished all the arches, carefully position the support (Stencil 12) centrally just underneath the point where the arches join.*

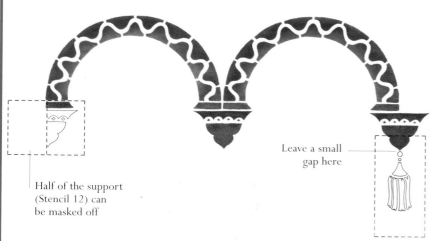

Half of the support (Stencil 12) can be masked off

4 *If you want to finish the line of arches neatly – for example, in a corner – mask off one half of the support stencil.*

Leave a small gap here

5 *Finish off the arches with the tassel motif. Place Stencil 15 just below the support and lightly dab in color.*

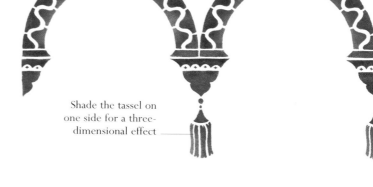

Shade the tassel on one side for a three-dimensional effect

6 *Use a plumb line if you want the tassels to hang straight, or position them at a slight angle to create a "windblown" effect.*

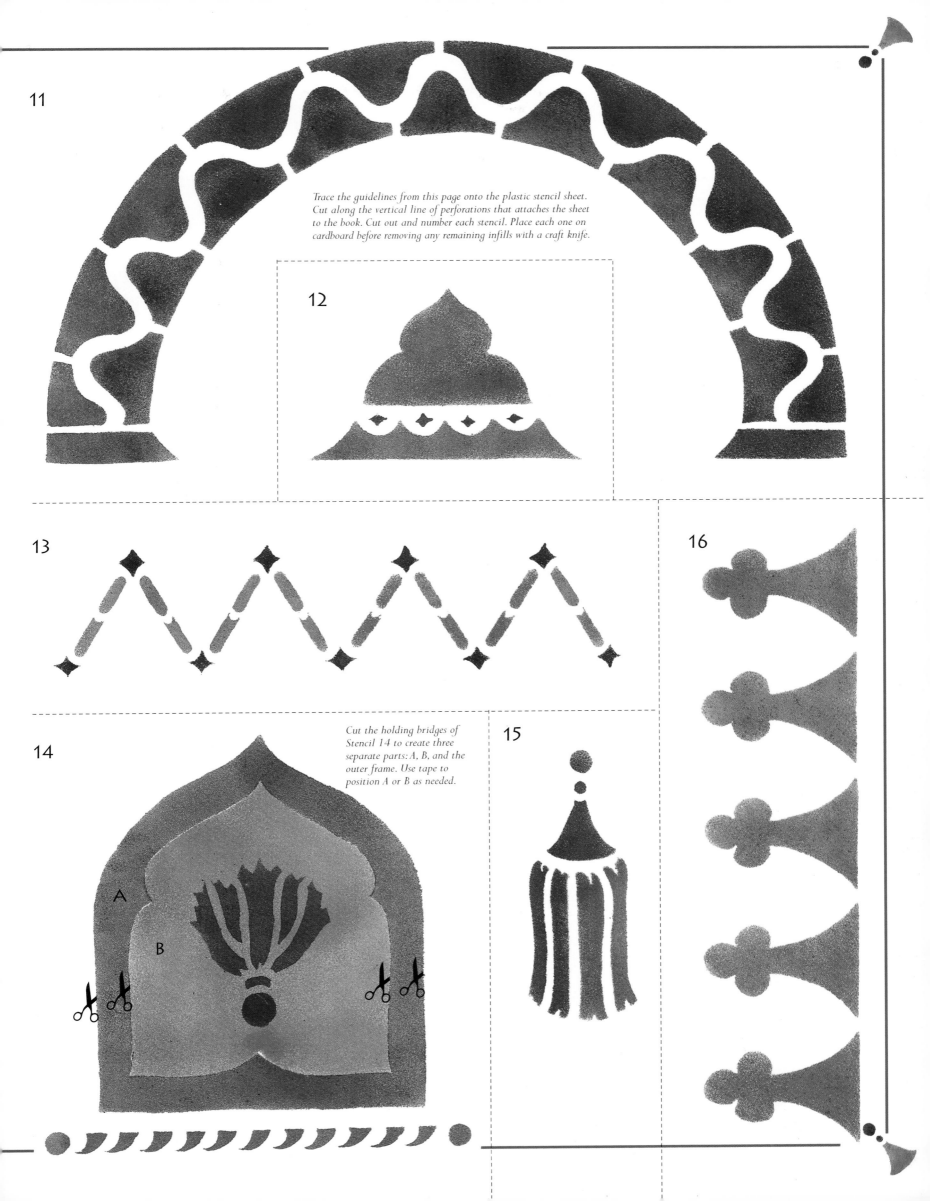

11

Trace the guidelines from this page onto the plastic stencil sheet. Cut along the vertical line of perforations that attaches the sheet to the book. Cut out and number each stencil. Place each one on cardboard before removing any remaining infills with a craft knife.

12

13

16

14

Cut the holding bridges of Stencil 14 to create three separate parts: A, B, and the outer frame. Use tape to position A or B as needed.

A

B

15

Moorish Variations

Single-Pawn Border: Stencil 16

Double-Pawn Border: Stencil 16

Try using this design above a baseboard or miter it around a picture frame

This mirrored design, with its interesting negative (interior) shape, creates the illusion of window tracery

Bells & Tassels: Stencils 12, 15

Braided Shields & Tassels: Stencils 14, 14a, 14b, 15

Triangles & Beaded Shields: Stencils 10, 13, 14, 14b

This is an excellent design for a valance above a window

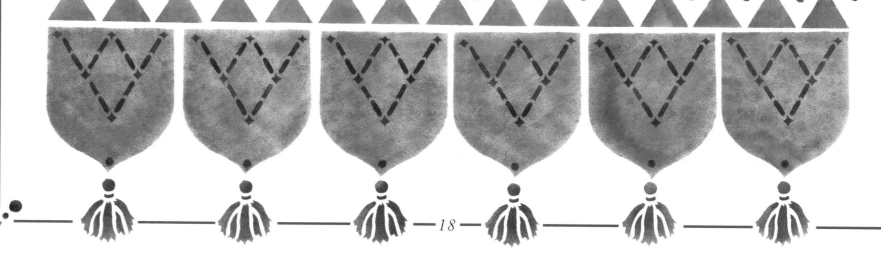

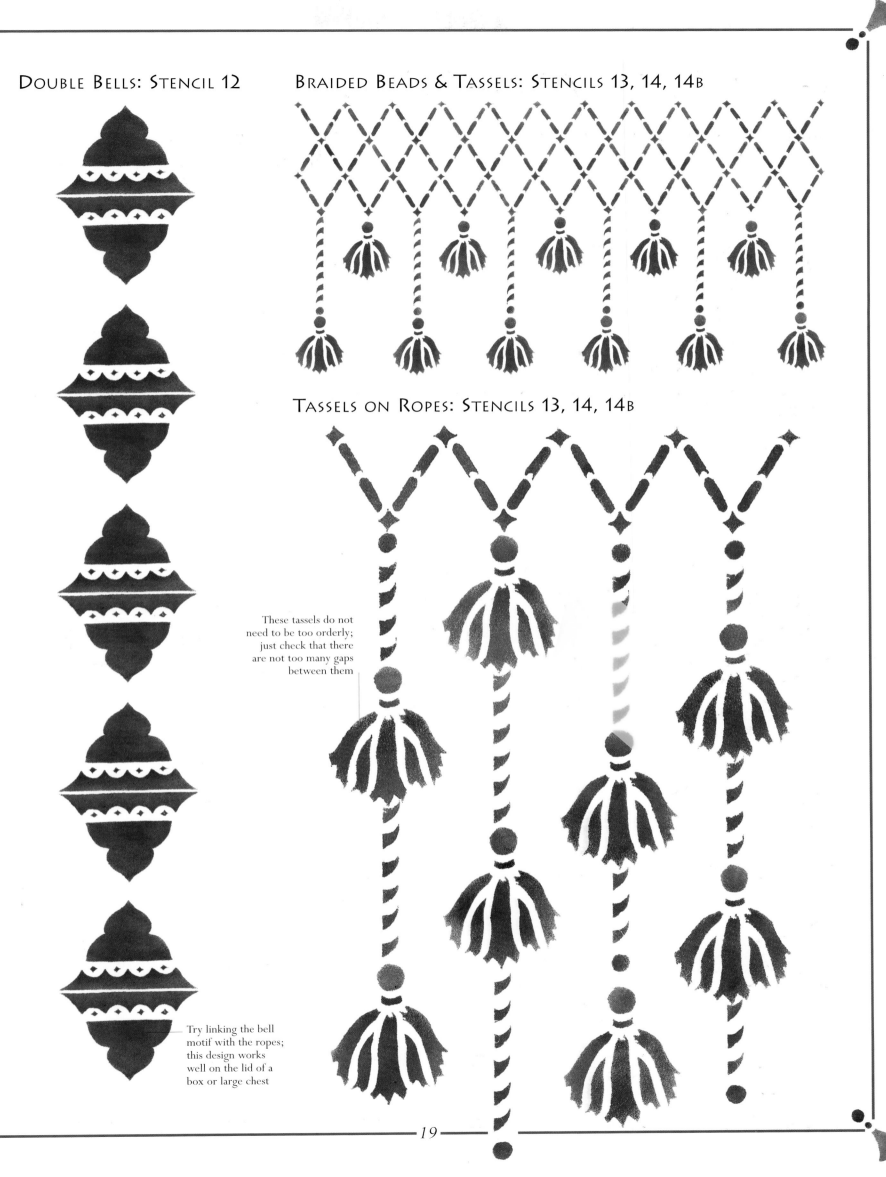

Double Bells: Stencil 12

Braided Beads & Tassels: Stencils 13, 14, 14b

Tassels on Ropes: Stencils 13, 14, 14b

These tassels do not need to be too orderly; just check that there are not too many gaps between them

Try linking the bell motif with the ropes; this design works well on the lid of a box or large chest

NATIVE AMERICAN

ABOUT 20,000 YEARS AGO, during the last Ice Age, hunters from Siberia crossed a land bridge into Alaska and later dispersed to form more than 300 Native American tribes. Many, especially those of the western Great Basin and Great Plains, remained nomads, living in buffalo-hide tipis decorated with paints made from ground stones, vegetable dyes, and earth pigments. The porcupine quills used to sew tipis were also dyed and stitched onto saddlebags and clothing to create elaborate designs. Native American belief was based on a profound respect for nature, and one of the most revered animals was the eagle. Universally linked with solar deities and a symbol of authority, strength, and pride, the eagle was called Thunderbird; its feathers represented rays of the sun and were attached to sacred ceremonial pipes, arrows, headdresses, and war shields.

When stenciling designs onto fabric, add a special medium to acrylic paints; quilt by hand or use a sewing machine to achieve a patchwork look.

Position carefully on the horizontal line marked out on the wall

1 Before painting the eagle frieze, practice on shelf or scrap paper; check the size of the pattern and repeat to make sure it fits the wall. Place Stencil 17 on a penciled horizontal line and create a border.

Position Stencil 19B in the center of the outer frame of Stencil 19, and attach to the surface with double-sided tape   Remove 19A

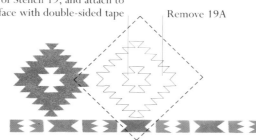

2 Take Stencil 19 and place it just above the border. With double-sided tape, attach 19B in the center. Stencil a row of diamonds along the border, making sure they are all the same distance apart.

3 Once you have completed one row of diamonds, make a second row just above the first, leaving the same gap between them as before. If you want a deeper frieze, stencil a third row of diamonds.

4 Mark a horizontal line above the diamonds, leaving the same space between the border and the diamonds as at the base of the frieze. Stencil the border.

Place the eagle motif between — but not touching — the diamonds

5 Now position the eagles (Stencil 21) in the spaces between the diamonds; pencil a horizontal line so that they line up evenly.

6 This is the completed eagle frieze, which would look striking on a wall or large chest. Experiment by combining the eagle and diamond with other stencils.

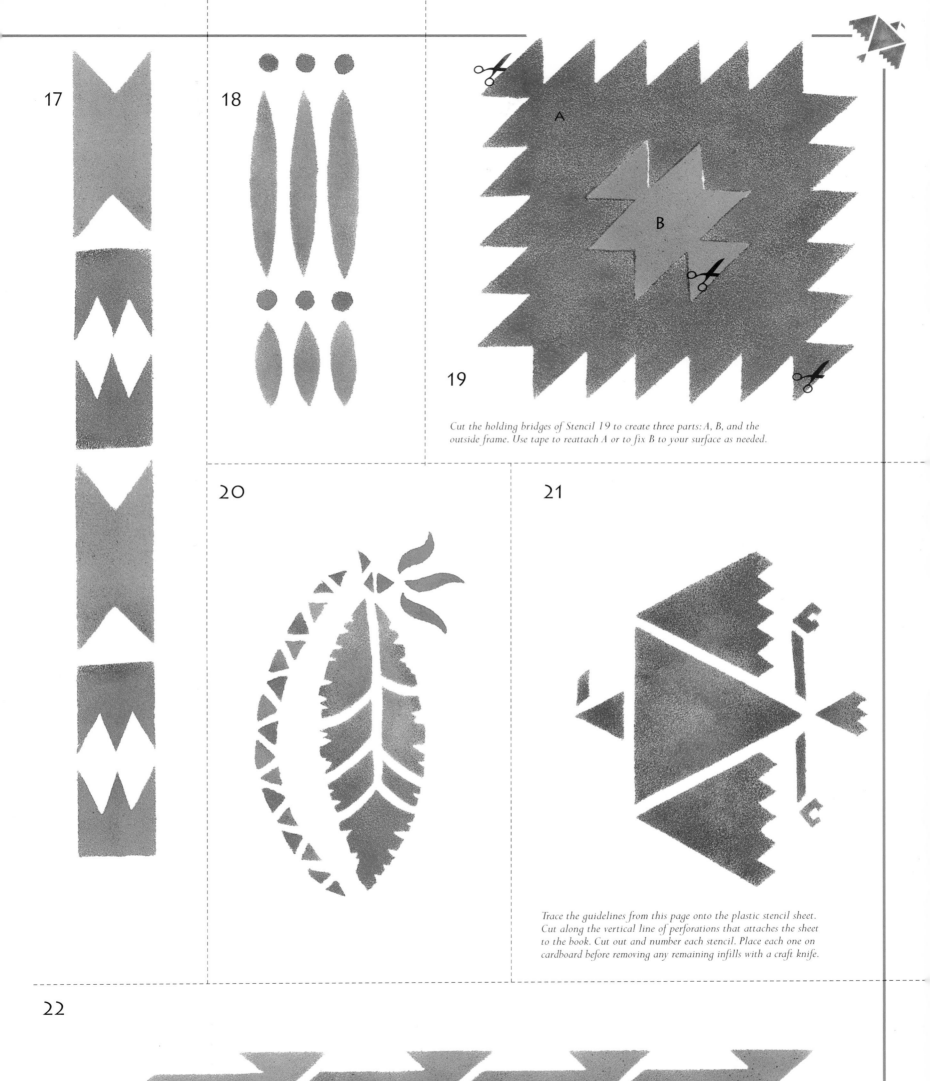

17

18

19

Cut the holding bridges of Stencil 19 to create three parts: A, B, and the outside frame. Use tape to reattach A or to fix B to your surface as needed.

20

21

Trace the guidelines from this page onto the plastic stencil sheet. Cut along the vertical line of perforations that attaches the sheet to the book. Cut out and number each stencil. Place each one on cardboard before removing any remaining infills with a craft knife.

22

Native American Variations

Eagle Feather & Porcupine Quill Border: Stencils 18, 20

Keep the baseline level, but angle the feathers for a more natural look

Wide Tomahawk Border: Stencil 22

This is an effective design for a dado rail, or to create vertical wall panels

Eagle Feather Border: Stencil 20

Use this design as a vertical motif on curtains or walls

Tomahawk & Diamond Frieze: Stencils 17, 19, 19a, 19b, 22

DIAMOND FRIEZE: STENCILS 9, 19

Position Stencil 19 on your surface, attach 19B (the small motif) in the center, and dab in paint to create the large diamond

BOXED DIAMOND FRIEZE: STENCILS 6, 19A, 30A

Attach Stencil 30A to the surface, place Stencil 19A in the center with some double-sided tape or blue tack, then dab in a bright or contrasting color in the center

TOMAHAWK BORDER: STENCIL 22

Mask Stencil 32 to create this design — change direction of the stripes at the midpoint of the border

BROW BAND BORDER: STENCILS 17, 32

DIAMOND & PORCUPINE QUILL BORDER: STENCILS 18, 19

Follow the instructions for the diamond frieze above, then remove 19B; reattach 19A inside the frame of Stencil 19 with tape, and dab in the small central motif

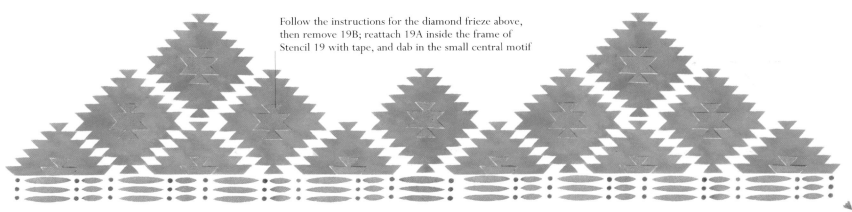

MAYAN & AZTEC

NTIL THE SIXTEENTH CENTURY, when they were overcome by the invading *conquistadores* from Spain, the Mayan and Aztec tribes dominated Central America. Their powerful, hierarchical culture derived from older Amerindian tribes who had been building stone and adobe stepped pyramids in the region from about 1800 BC; these buildings are the source of the recurring step motif. One tribe, the Toltecs, built stone temples at Tula that are remarkable for the way in which are they fitted together without cement. All these cultures held elaborate religious festivals for their hundreds of gods. Their ceremonial costumes incorporated gems, parrot feathers, and the long, streaming tailfeathers of the quetzal bird associated with a major deity, Quetzalcoatl, the plumed serpent god of wisdom. The torches that were used in these ceremonies are another popular motif.

These stencils have been used on natural woven baskets. Try using them on rush mats or cane blinds.

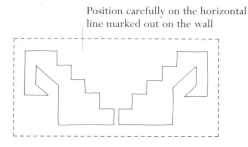

Position carefully on the horizontal line marked out on the wall

Shade around the edges of Stencil 25

The finished plume and dots

You could also use a vibrant, contrasting color for this motif

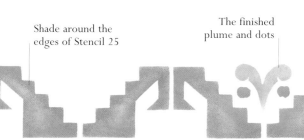

1 *Using a level, mark out a horizontal line on the wall. Mask off the central plume motif on Stencil 25, place the stencil on the line, and dab in color.*

2 *Continue to stencil the step motif along the horizontal line, leaving a small gap between the two. This gap can be increased if you want to stretch the design.*

3 *Once you have completed the border, mask off Stencil 23 to reveal only the central plume motif and dots. Center the stencil between the steps, and dab in paint.*

The tips of the finished motif are shaded with flamelike colors

Use a plumb line or level to keep the torches straight

Mask off the torch so that only the top flame section is shown

4 *Position Stencil 24, the feather plume, above the last stencil, leaving a small gap. If you flip the plume and stencil from the other side, you can vary the look.*

5 *Paint in the torch (Stencil 27) in the spaces between the feather plumes. Then mask off the top section of the stencil, and fill in the gaps at the base of the steps.*